The Power Guide to Empowering Kids to Improve Reading Comprehension

Table of Contents

Introduction 2

Chapter 1: Understanding Chunking 5

Chapter 2: Modeling the Chunking Process 8

Chapter 3: Highlighting or Underlining (Annotating) Key Information with Notes 13

Chapter 4 : Using Graphic Organizers to Visualize Chunks and Relationships 17

Chapter 5: Guided Practice 23

Chapter 6: Signal Words - Unlocking the Key to Conquer Complex Texts 33

Chapter 7: Symbols and Abbreviations - Unlocking Efficiency in Reading 37

Chapter 8: Collaborative Discussions - Amplifying Understanding Through Shared Chunks, Signal Words, and Symbols 40

Chapter 9: Real-World Application - Bridging Reading Strategies to Everyday Scenarios 44

Chapter 10: Differentiated Instruction - Tailoring Chunking Strategies to Individual Needs 48

Chapter 11: Independent Practice Chunking with Short Passages 51

Chapter 12: Independent Practice Chunking with Long Passages 54

Chapter 13: Chunking Non-linear Passages 60

Chapter 14: Overcoming Challenges in Chunking 63

Chapter 15: Home-School Connection - Extending Chunking Strategies beyond the Classroom 67

Appendix: Additional resources, activities, and worksheets for practicing chunking skills 71

Introduction

As an educator, my primary goal has always been to foster a love for reading in children and equip them with essential skills that would empower them for a lifetime. Over the years, I have witnessed countless students struggle with comprehending and retaining information while reading. It became apparent to me that a breakthrough was needed to overcome this hurdle.

This realization led me on a journey of research, experimentation, and collaboration with fellow educators and reading specialists. The culmination of this endeavor is my book, **The Power of Chunking: A Guide to Empowering Kids to Improve Reading Comprehension**. In this book, I aim to provide teachers, parents, and students with a comprehensive guide to an effective reading strategy called chunking.

The concept of chunking, when applied to reading, involves breaking down a passage or text into smaller, more manageable sections or chunks. By doing so, we can enhance comprehension, boost retention, and ultimately, improve overall reading skills. This approach has proven to be a powerful tool in helping students make significant progress in their reading abilities.

In **The Power of Chunking**, I will not only delve into the theoretical framework behind this strategy but also provide step-by-step instructions and practical examples to help educators implement chunking in their classrooms. Furthermore, this book is designed with parents in mind, offering valuable insights into how they can support their children in developing strong reading comprehension skills at home.

One of the unique aspects of this book is its focus on empowering children in the learning process. By teaching students to chunk passages effectively, they are equipped with a valuable tool that enables them to take control of their own learning journey. When children grasp the power of chunking, they gain confidence, improve their reading skills, and develop a lifelong love for reading.

I am excited to share The Power of Chunking with educators, parents, and anyone passionate about nurturing young readers. By utilizing this strategy, we can create a positive and engaging learning environment that cultivates strong reading comprehension skills in children.I aim to provide a straightforward, step-by-step guide to the effective reading strategy of chunking. By breaking down a passage or text into smaller, more manageable sections, students can enhance comprehension, boost retention, and improve overall reading skills.

Chapter 1: Understanding Chunking 📚

Chunking is a powerful reading comprehension strategy that involves organizing information into meaningful units or "chunks." In this chapter, we will explore the definition of chunking and its relevance to reading comprehension. Additionally, we will discuss the benefits of chunking passages and how it enhances our understanding of the text.

Definition of Chunking

When we refer to chunking in the context of reading comprehension, we mean breaking down information into smaller, manageable parts. These parts, or chunks, are easier to process and remember, allowing for better understanding of the overall text. Chunking involves grouping related ideas or concepts together, helping us make sense of complex information.

Relevance of Chunking to Reading Comprehension

Chunking plays a vital role in enhancing reading comprehension in multiple ways. By breaking information into smaller chunks, we are better able to grasp the main ideas, identify key details, and understand the relationships between different parts of a passage.

One primary benefit of chunking is that it aids in overcoming the limitations of working memory. Our ability to hold and process information in our working memory is limited. By chunking information, we can effectively optimize our working memory capacity, allowing us to process more information efficiently.

Chunking also promotes better reading fluency. By organizing information into chunks, readers can navigate through the text more smoothly and coherently. This reduces the cognitive load and promotes a better flow of comprehension.

Furthermore, chunking improves our ability to extract important information from a passage. By identifying and grouping related ideas, we can better discern the main concepts and supporting details, enabling us to comprehend the text's central message more accurately.

Understanding chunking is essential for improving reading comprehension. By defining what chunking is and highlighting its relevance to reading comprehension, we have established a foundation for further exploration. We have also discussed the benefits of chunking passages and how it enhances our understanding of the text. As we delve deeper into the topic, we will explore various chunking techniques and strategies that can be applied to different types of texts, guiding us towards becoming more efficient and effective readers.

Chapter 2: Modeling the Chunking Process 🎯 ✂

To effectively demonstrate the chunking process, it is crucial to start by reading a passage aloud and pausing at natural breaks or transitions. This modeling technique allows students to visually and audibly comprehend the concept of chunking.

By deliberately pausing at appropriate points in the passage, students can see how the text naturally divides into smaller, more manageable sections. These pauses are typically at places where there is a change in topic, idea, or shift in the narrative structure.

During this modeling phase, it is essential to explain that chunking is not about randomly dividing the text but about identifying and understanding the flow and structure of the content. By doing so, students will be able to grasp the main idea and supporting details within each chunk more effectively.

Example:

Step 1: Let's consider the following passage:

"The rain was pouring down outside, and the wind howled through the trees. Inside, the cozy fireplace crackled, spreading warmth throughout the room. Lucy cuddled up on the couch, engrossed in her favorite book."

When reading this passage aloud, you would pause after the first sentence: "The rain was pouring down outside, and the wind howled through the trees." This represents the first chunk.

After that, you would pause again: "Inside, the cozy fireplace crackled, spreading warmth throughout the room." This represents the second chunk.

Finally, you would pause for the last time: "Lucy cuddled up on the couch, engrossed in her favorite book." This represents the third and final chunk.

By demonstrating the chunking process in this way, you are enabling students to observe and understand the natural breaks or transitions within the text, which are essential for effective chunking.

This step sets the foundation for the subsequent stages, where students actively engage in applying the chunking strategy by identifying the main idea and supporting details within each chunk.

Next, let's delve into Step 2 to further enhance students' comprehension and analytic skills.

Step 2: Identifying the Main Idea and Supporting Details

After modeling the chunking process, the next step is for students to actively use the strategy by identifying the main idea and supporting details within each chunk.

The main idea is the primary message conveyed in the text, while supporting details are the specific information or evidence that supports and enhances the main idea. It is crucial to explain to students that identifying the main idea and supporting details promotes a deeper understanding of the text and allows them to make connections between different parts of the passage.

Example:

Let's consider the same passage we used in Step 1:

Chunk 1:

"The rain was pouring down outside, and the wind howled through the trees."

Chunk 2:

"Inside, the cozy fireplace crackled, spreading warmth throughout the room."

Chunk 3:

"Lucy cuddled up on the couch, engrossed in her favorite book."

In Chunk 1, the main idea is the weather conditions outside, with the rain pouring down and the wind howling. The supporting details are these specific weather conditions, such as the pouring rain and howling wind. Students should ask themselves, "What is this chunk all about?", and the answer should be, the weather outside.

In Chunk 2, the main idea is the cozy atmosphere inside the room, created by the crackling fireplace. The supporting detail is the warmth spreading throughout the room. Students should ask themselves, "What is this chunk all about?", and the answer should be, the comfort and warmth of the room.

In Chunk 3, the main idea is Lucy's engagement with her favorite book. The supporting detail is her cuddling up on the couch. Students should ask themselves, "What is this chunk all about?", and the answer should be, Lucy's interest and engagement in reading.

By actively engaging in chunking and identifying the main idea and supporting details, students gain a deeper understanding of the text. This approach enhances critical thinking and analysis skills and fosters a love for learning and reading.

Chapter 3: Highlighting or Underlining (Annotating) Key Information with Notes

In addition to the chunking process, teaching students to physically highlight or underline key phrases, main ideas, or supporting details in a passage is an effective strategy known as annotating. This technique aids in visually separating chunks and helps students identify important information within a text. Taking it a step further, students can add notes alongside these annotations to support their comprehension and analysis.

Step-by-Step Process:

1. Introduce students to the concept of annotation and explain its purpose. Annotation involves marking or highlighting significant information within a passage to aid comprehension and analysis. Emphasize that adding notes alongside annotations further enhances understanding.
2. Provide students with a passage or text to read. It can be a short paragraph or an excerpt from a longer piece.

3. Teach students how to identify key phrases, main ideas, and supporting details. Explain that these are the elements they should focus on while reading and annotating. Emphasize the importance of notating their thoughts and insights as they annotate.
4. Model the annotation process by reading the passage aloud and demonstrating how to identify and mark the key information through underlining or highlighting. Additionally, model the process of adding notes alongside the annotations to further explain or clarify their thoughts.

Example:

Let's use the same passage from previous steps as an example:

"The rain was pouring down outside, and the wind howled through the trees. Inside, the cozy fireplace crackled, spreading warmth throughout the room. Lucy cuddled up on the couch, engrossed in her favorite book."

After reading the passage aloud, guide students on how to annotate key information and add notes alongside their annotations. For instance, they might choose to annotate and add notes:

- In Chunk 1: *Annotation*: "the rain pouring down outside" and "the wind howled through the trees." *Note*: "Creates a sense of a stormy atmosphere."
- In Chunk 2: *Annotation*: "the cozy fireplace crackled" and "spreading warmth throughout the room." *Note*: "Contrast between the storm outside and the cozy atmosphere inside."
- In Chunk 3: *Annotation*: "Lucy cuddled up on the couch" and "engrossed in her favorite book." *Note*: "Highlights Lucy's comfort and engagement with the story."

By combining annotations with notes, students not only visually separate the chunks and identify important information but also provide explanations or insights that support their understanding of the text.

Encourage students to share and discuss their annotations and notes with peers. This can be done through small-group or whole-class discussions. Encouraging dialogue and multiple perspectives fosters a deeper understanding of the text and allows students to learn from one another.

In conclusion, teaching students to physically highlight or underline key phrases, main ideas, or supporting details in a passage through annotation, and adding notes alongside those annotations, assists in visually separating chunks and identifying important information. This comprehensive annotation process deepens students' comprehension, encourages critical thinking, and strengthens their analytical skills.

Chapter 4 : Using Graphic Organizers to Visualize Chunks and Relationships 📖🔍

Graphic organizers are powerful tools that help students visually represent the different chunks and relationships within a passage. By using graphic organizers such as flowcharts, concept maps, or Venn diagrams, students can organize their thoughts, make connections between ideas, and gain a deeper understanding of the text. Encouraging students to label each chunk using symbols or icons further enhances their comprehension by clearly indicating the main ideas or supporting details.

Step-by-Step Process:

1. Introduce students to different types of graphic organizers commonly used to represent chunks and relationships:
    - **Flowcharts**: Flowcharts are visual representations that use arrows and boxes to show the sequence of ideas or events. They are especially useful when explaining processes or illustrating cause and effect relationships.

- **Concept maps**: Concept maps visually depict relationships between ideas or concepts using circles or bubbles connected by lines. They allow students to demonstrate their understanding of concepts and how they are related to each other.
- **Venn diagrams**: Venn diagrams use overlapping circles to compare and contrast ideas or concepts. They are especially useful when discussing similarities and differences between two or more items.

2. Provide students with an example passage and the graphic organizer of their choice (flowchart, concept map, or Venn diagram). Explain that they will use the graphic organizer to represent the different chunks and relationships within the passage.
3. Model how to use the selected graphic organizer to represent the chunks and relationships within the passage. Show students how to label each chunk using symbols or icons that indicate the main ideas or supporting details.

Example:

Let's use the same passage for this example:

"The rain was pouring down outside, and the wind howled through the trees. Inside, the cozy fireplace crackled, spreading warmth throughout the room. Lucy cuddled up on the couch, engrossed in her favorite book."

Here's an example of how students can represent this passage using different graphic organizers:

1. **Flowchart:**

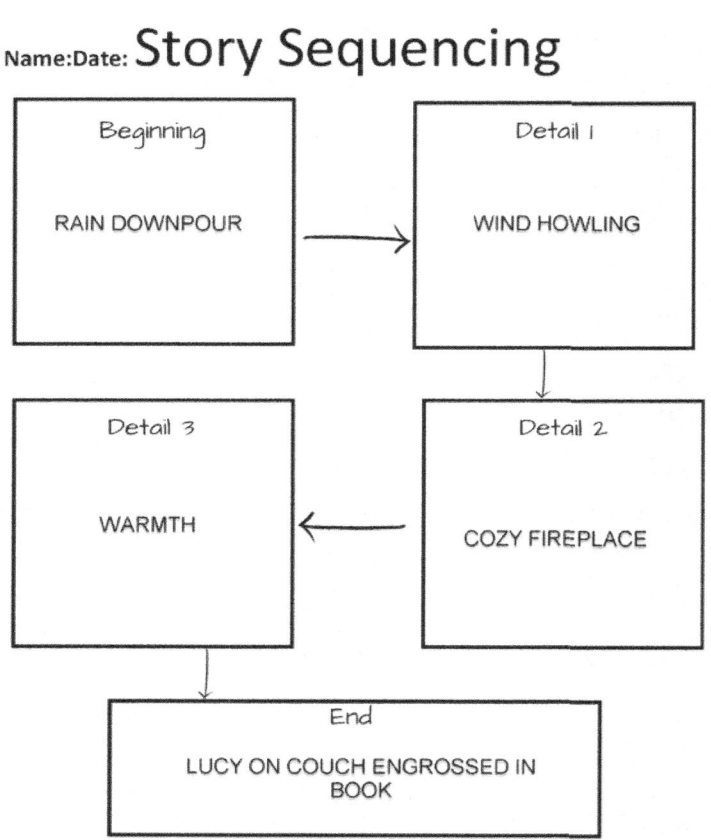

In this flowchart, the main ideas and supporting details flow in a linear sequence, representing the chunks of the passage.

2. **Concept Map:**

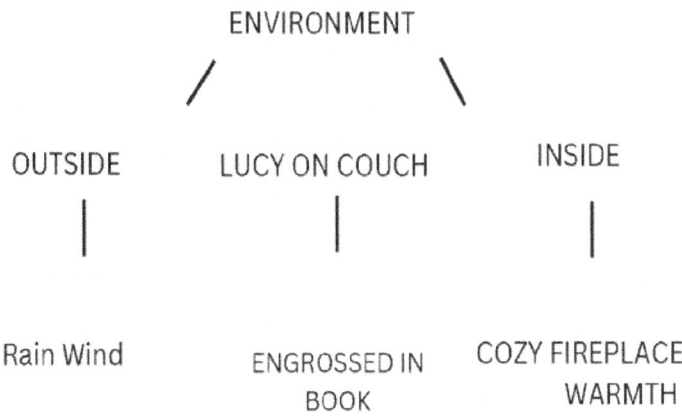

In this concept map, the main idea of the passage ("ENVIRONMENT") branches out to the different chunks, demonstrating the relationships between them.

3. **Venn Diagram:**

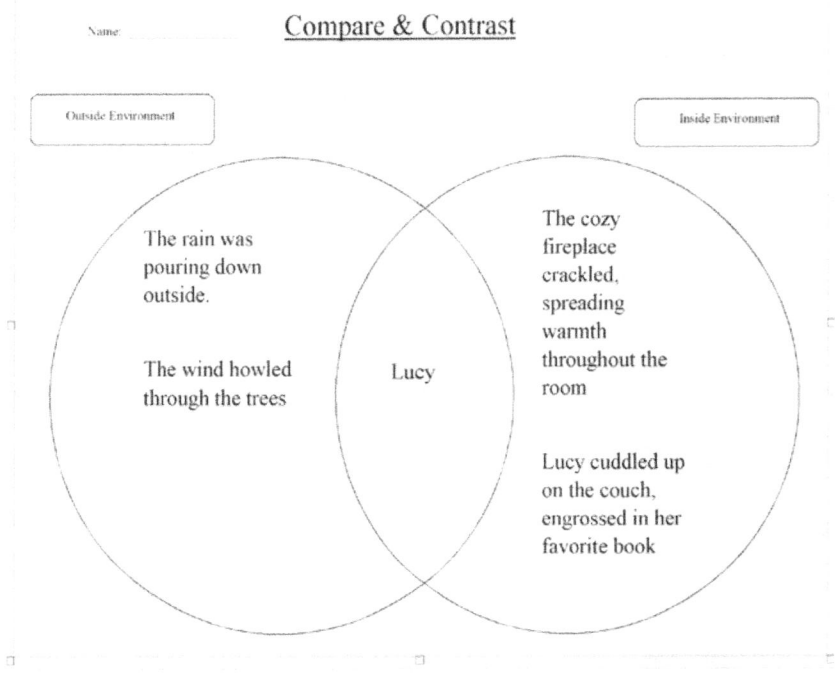

In this Venn diagram, the overlapping circles represent the similarities and differences between the different environments ("OUTSIDE" and "INSIDE") described in the passage.

Encourage students to create their own graphic organizers based on the passage, using symbols or icons to represent each chunk. They should label each chunk with key phrases or main ideas to further enhance their understanding and analysis of the text.

Explain that the choice of graphic organizer depends on the type of information being represented and the preferences of the student. Encourage students to experiment with different types of graphic organizers to find the one that works best for them.

In conclusion, utilizing graphic organizers such as flowcharts, concept maps, or Venn diagrams is a valuable strategy to help students visually represent the different chunks and relationships within a passage. By labeling each chunk with symbols or icons, students can clearly indicate the main ideas and supporting details, further enhancing their comprehension and analysis of the text.

Chapter 5: Guided Practice 🍎✏️🤝

In this chapter, we will delve into guided practice activities that provide structured guidance and support for students as they practice chunking passages. These activities are designed to help students develop their chunking skills and gradually become proficient in chunking independently.

Activity 1: Chunking Worksheets

To begin, we will provide students with chunking worksheets that contain passages for analysis. These worksheets will include instructions and prompts to guide students through the chunking process. The passages chosen for the worksheets will vary in complexity, allowing students to practice chunking in different contexts.

At first, the worksheets will have more scaffolding and support. The instructions will explicitly guide students to identify natural breaks or transitions in the text and divide the passage into chunks. Prompts will also be provided to help students identify the main ideas and supporting details within each chunk.

As students become more proficient in chunking, the level of scaffolding will gradually decrease. The worksheets will provide less explicit guidance, encouraging students to rely more on their own analysis and decision-making skills. This progression ensures that students gradually develop their independence in chunking passages.

Let's Practice:

Worksheet 1: Fiction Passage

Title: "The Mysterious Island"

Instructions: Read the passage below and identify natural breaks or transitions in the text. Divide the passage into chunks and label each chunk. Then, write the main idea and supporting details for each chunk.

Passage:
"Emily and her friends set off on their adventure to the mysterious island. The boat rocked gently as they approached the shore, filled with excitement and curiosity. As they stepped onto the island, they were greeted by lush vegetation and vibrant colors. The first chunk of their exploration was to analyze the plant life and identify any unique species. They carefully examined each leaf and took notes on their observations. Suddenly, a rustling sound came from behind them, and they turned to see a group of colorful birds flying overhead. This unexpected encounter

became the second chunk of their exploration, as they observed the birds in their natural habitat and documented their behaviors. Finally, as the sun began to set, Emily and her friends found a cozy spot and decided to rest. They reflected on the day's adventures and made plans for tomorrow, which marked the third and final chunk of their exploration."

Chunk 1:

- Main Idea:
- Supporting Details:

Chunk 2:

- Main Idea:
- Supporting Details:

Chunk 3:

- Main Idea:
- Supporting Details:

Worksheet 2: Non-Fiction Passage

Title: "The Importance of Recycling"

Instructions: Read the passage below and identify natural breaks or transitions in the text. Divide the passage into chunks and label each chunk. Then, write the main idea and supporting details for each chunk.

Passage:

"Recycling plays a crucial role in preserving the environment. The first chunk of the recycling process is sorting. Sorting involves separating different types of recyclable materials, such as plastic, glass, and paper. Once the materials are sorted, they are then sent for processing. This becomes the second chunk of the recycling process, where the recyclables are cleaned and prepared for reuse. Recycling facilities use specialized machinery and techniques to convert these materials into new products. The third and final chunk of the recycling process is the production of new items using the recycled materials. This step involves manufacturing and creating new products from the processed recyclables. By completing this cycle, recycling reduces waste, conserves resources, and helps protect the planet."

Chunk 1:

- Main Idea:
- Supporting Details:

Chunk 2:

- Main Idea:
- Supporting Details:

Chunk 3:

- Main Idea:

- Supporting Details:

Worksheet 3: Historical Passage

Title: "The American Revolution"

Instructions: Read the passage below and identify natural breaks or transitions in the text. Divide the passage into chunks and label each chunk. Then, write the main idea and supporting details for each chunk.

Passage:
"The American Revolution marked a turning point in history. The first chunk of the revolution was the build-up to the conflict. Tensions grew between Britain and the thirteen American colonies due to issues such as taxation and representation. This lead to the second chunk, the outbreak of the revolution. Starting with the battles of Lexington and Concord, the colonists fought for their independence from British rule. As the revolution progressed, the third chunk emerged, the formation of a new government. Led by individuals like George Washington and Thomas Jefferson, the colonists established the foundations of the United States of America. The American Revolution brought about significant changes and ideals that remain influential to this day."

Chunk 1:

- Main Idea:

- Supporting Details:

Chunk 2:

- Main Idea:
- Supporting Details:

Chunk 3:

- Main Idea:
- Supporting Details:

These chunking worksheets provide students with different types of passages to practice their chunking skills. As they progress, encourage students to gradually rely more on their analysis and decision-making skills, developing their independence in chunking passages.

Activity 2: Collaborative Chunking Exercises

Objective: To provide guided practice in collaborative chunking exercises to enhance students' chunking skills and promote effective group discussion.

Materials:

- Sample passage handouts (fiction, non-fiction, historical, etc.)
- Sticky notes or index cards

- Markers or pens
- Pairs or small groups of students
- Teacher or facilitator guidance and support

Instructions:

1. Provide pairs or small groups of students with a sample passage handout.
2. Instruct students to work collaboratively, analyzing and chunking the passage together. Encourage them to use sticky notes or index cards to mark the natural breaks in the text.
3. Prompt each group to discuss the main ideas and supporting details within each chunk. Remind them to consider the flow and organization of the passage and make connections between different sections.
4. As students work, circulate among the groups, providing guidance and support. Encourage them to explain their thought process and engage in meaningful discussions within their groups.
5. Gradually decrease the level of guidance and support as students gain more confidence and proficiency. Allow them to take ownership of their chunking analysis and collaborate with their peers effectively.
6. Once the groups finish chunking the passage, regather as a whole group and have each group share their chunks, main ideas, and supporting

details. Encourage other groups to ask questions or provide feedback.
7. Facilitate a discussion to compare and contrast the different approaches taken by each group. Discuss the reasoning behind the chunking decisions, as well as the similarities and differences in the main ideas and supporting details.

By engaging in collaborative chunking exercises, students can enhance their analytical thinking, discussion skills, and comprehension abilities. These exercises promote effective group discussion, allowing students to learn from each other's perspectives and insights. Gradually decreasing the level of guidance and support empowers students to take ownership of their chunking analysis and builds their confidence and proficiency in the process.

Activity 3: Chunking Reflection and Feedback

Objective: To provide opportunities for students to reflect on their chunking process and receive feedback on their analysis skills.

Instructions:

1. After students complete each guided practice activity, create space for reflection and feedback.
2. Encourage students to reflect on their chunking process and identify areas for improvement. Ask questions such as:

- What strategies did you use to identify the natural breaks in the text?
- Did you feel confident in your ability to analyze each chunk? Why or why not?
- Were there any challenges or difficulties you encountered during the process?
- How could you improve your chunking analysis in the future?

3. Have students reflect on the effectiveness of their analysis in terms of grasping the main ideas and supporting details within each chunk. Ask questions such as:
    - Did you accurately identify the main ideas and supporting details of each chunk?
    - Did your analysis help you understand the overall meaning of the passage?
    - Were there any instances where you missed important information or misunderstood the main ideas?
    - What strategies could you use to improve your comprehension and analysis skills?
4. Provide feedback to students on their chunking analysis. Highlight their strengths and offer specific suggestions for improvement. Focus on the accuracy and clarity of their chunking process, as well as their ability to identify the main ideas and supporting details. Use a constructive and supportive approach to encourage growth and development.

5. Throughout the guided practice activities, monitor students' progress and provide individualized support as needed. Address any misconceptions or challenges students may face and provide guidance to help them build their chunking skills effectively.

By incorporating reflection and feedback into the chunking activities, students can learn from their experiences and make adjustments to improve their analysis skills. This process supports their development as proficient chunkers, enhancing their reading comprehension abilities.

Chapter 6: Signal Words - Unlocking the Key to Conquer Complex Texts 🔑📚

Have you ever started reading a passage only to become lost within its intricacies? The text may have seemed like a jumbled mess of ideas, making it difficult to identify the main ideas and supporting details. But what if we told you that there is a way to make sense of even the most complex texts? Enter signal words - the key to unlocking the structure and organization of written works.

Signal words or phrases are crucial indicators that help readers identify transitions, comparisons, and conclusions within a text. These linguistic signposts provide guidance for readers and make it easier to understand complex and interconnected ideas. Whether you are reading a novel, a science textbook, or a newspaper article, signal words are always present, awaiting discovery.

Some examples of signal words include transitional words like "however," "although," "on the other hand," "in contrast," and "nevertheless" that indicate a shift from one idea to another. Other signal words and phrases indicate comparison, for example, "similarly," "likewise," "just as," or "in the same way," while "on the contrary," "conversely," and "in comparison" indicate differences. Lastly, signal words indicating a conclusion include "in summary," "in conclusion," and "therefore."

Recognizing these signal words and phrases can significantly benefit young readers in multiple ways. By identifying and understanding signal words, children can immediately focus on the most critical parts of a text. Encourage them to pause and reflect upon encountering these words or phrases, which will help them recognize the need for chunking - breaking down complex texts into more manageable parts.

Additionally, signal words can help students identify the author's intended meaning and writing style. Every writer has a unique style, and understanding how they use signal words can provide insight into their work. Learning how to analyze and interpret what authors mean by different signal words and phrases can also be an important part of developing critical thinking skills.

Another benefit of learning about signal words is that it can help students with writing. By recognizing signal words, children can learn how to structure their own writing in a clear and organized way, making it easier for readers to understand and follow their ideas. Furthermore, they can add more signal words or phrases to their writing to create clear connections between their ideas.

In conclusion, signal words are an essential part of reading and writing. They help guide readers through complex texts, identifying significant transitions, comparisons, and conclusions. By teaching children to identify signal words, we can help them become more confident readers and writers, able to tackle even the most challenging texts with ease. So, let's continue to encourage our little ones to recognize and understand signal words, unlocking the keys to success in reading and writing!

Here is a list of signal words or phrases that indicate transitions, comparisons, or conclusions:

Transitions:

- However
- Although
- On the other hand
- In contrast
- Nevertheless
- Yet
- Whereas
- In comparison
- Similarly
- Likewise

Comparisons:

- Similarly
- Likewise
- Just as
- In the same way
- Equally
- As well as
- Also
- Compared to
- In a similar vein
- Correspondingly

Conclusions:

- In summary
- In conclusion
- Therefore
- Thus
- Hence
- Consequently
- As a result
- Ultimately
- To summarize
- For these reasons

It is important to note that this is not an exhaustive list, but it provides a good starting point for recognizing signal words or phrases that indicate transitions, comparisons, or conclusions in a text.

Chapter 7: Symbols and Abbreviations - Unlocking Efficiency in Reading 📚💥

In the quest to become proficient readers, it is essential to find creative and efficient ways to navigate through texts. One useful strategy is the use of symbols and abbreviations to represent common ideas or concepts. By introducing simple symbols or abbreviations, we can enhance comprehension and make the reading process more streamlined. Let's explore how these tools can revolutionize reading!

Symbols and abbreviations act as visual shortcuts that help readers quickly identify and remember important information. For example, an arrow can represent cause and effect, visually illustrating the relationship between two ideas. Similarly, an asterisk can signify an important detail that should be given extra attention. By incorporating symbols such as these into one's reading practice, it becomes easier to grasp the main ideas and supporting details within a text.

To fully leverage symbols and abbreviations, it is helpful to create a key or legend that acts as a reference guide while chunking passages. This key can define the symbols and abbreviations used, making it easier to remember their meanings and apply them consistently. Encouraging children to create their own unique symbols or abbreviations further enhances their engagement and ownership of the reading process.

Let's explore some common symbols and abbreviations that can be utilized:

1. → = Indicates cause and effect.
2. ! = Represents an important detail or point.
3. ✓ = Signifies agreement or support for an idea.
4. ▶ = Highlights a key point or idea.
5. ↔ = Denotes a comparison or contrast between two concepts.
6. ✯ = Marks an interesting or noteworthy fact.
7. ✗ = Indicates a significant point or idea that should be remembered.

By using these symbols alongside key abbreviations, readers can significantly improve their reading efficiency. Abbreviations allow for the representation of long or frequently occurring words, reducing cognitive load and increasing reading fluency. Here are some examples of useful abbreviations:

1. b/c = Because
2. w/ = With

3. e.g. = For example
4. etc. = Et cetera, meaning "and so on"
5. gov't = Government
6. avg. = Average
7. approx. = Approximately

When combined with symbols, these abbreviations help create a concise and easily understandable system for processing information. Students can be encouraged to create their own personalized symbols and abbreviations as well, tailored to their own reading preferences and comprehension needs.

In conclusion, symbols and abbreviations are powerful tools that contribute to efficient and effective reading. By introducing these visual shortcuts, readers can quickly identify and remember important information, enhancing their comprehension and retention. Creating a key or legend to refer to while chunking passages further reinforces the understanding and application of symbols and abbreviations. Let's encourage our young readers to embrace these strategies, unlocking a whole new level of reading efficiency and enjoyment! 📚💡

Chapter 8: Collaborative Discussions - Amplifying Understanding Through Shared Chunks, Signal Words, and Symbols

Reading is not merely a solitary activity; it thrives when shared and discussed. Engaging students in small-group or paired discussions can significantly enhance their understanding and retention of information. By giving them a platform to share their chunks, signal words, and symbols with their classmates, we create an environment that fosters collaboration and deeper comprehension. Let's dive into the power of collaborative discussions and how they can elevate the reading experience!

Small group or paired discussions provide students with an opportunity to articulate and exchange their ideas, thoughts, and insights. Encourage students to share their chunks, signal words, and symbols with their peers, fostering a rich and diverse exchange of perspectives. As they explain their thought process and reasoning behind their choices, students not only solidify their own understanding but also gain valuable insights from their classmates' interpretations.

During these discussions, it is crucial to create a safe and inclusive space where all voices are heard and respected. Encourage active listening and the sharing of constructive feedback. By doing so, students learn from one another and build upon their collective knowledge, creating a dynamic collaborative learning environment.

Here are some effective strategies to facilitate collaborative discussions:

1. Arrange small groups or pairs: Divide the class into smaller groups or pairs, ensuring that each student has an opportunity to engage actively in the discussion. This format promotes focused and meaningful conversations.

2. Set discussion goals: Provide students with specific goals or questions to guide their discussions. These goals can include analyzing the structure of a text, identifying main ideas and supporting details, or evaluating the effectiveness of a writer's argument. This focus encourages students to dig deeper into the text and have fruitful discussions.

3. Encourage active participation: Encourage all students to actively contribute to the discussion by asking open-ended questions and inviting multiple perspectives. Ensure that quieter students have an opportunity to share their thoughts, fostering an inclusive environment where everyone feels valued.

4. Use accountable talk protocols: Introduce accountable talk protocols that encourage students to actively listen, build on each other's ideas, and justify their reasoning. Teach them phrases such as "I agree with ___ because___" or "I respectfully disagree with ___ because___." These protocols promote critical thinking and respectful dialogue.

5. Provide guiding prompts: Offer guiding prompts that help students delve deeper into their chunks, signal words, and symbols. Prompt them to explain why they chose a particular symbol or signal word and how it contributes to their understanding of the text. These prompts encourage metacognition and reflection.

By engaging in collaborative discussions, students develop a deeper understanding of texts, improve their communication skills, and gain new perspectives. They also enhance their ability to analyze and evaluate information, building critical thinking skills that extend far beyond the realm of reading.

In conclusion, collaborative discussions provide an invaluable platform for students to share and expand their understanding of texts. By engaging in small-group or paired discussions, students can exchange their chunks, signal words, and symbols, fostering a collaborative learning environment. These discussions empower students to explain their thinking, listen actively, and learn from their peers. Let us encourage and facilitate these discussions, recognizing them as catalysts for growth, empathy, and enhanced reading comprehension. Together, we can unlock the full potential of our students' reading journeys!

Chapter 9: Real-World Application - Bridging Reading Strategies to Everyday Scenarios 🌍📚💡

The skills of chunking information and using signals and symbols are not limited to the pages of a textbook; they have practical applications in our everyday lives as well. It is essential to connect these reading strategies to real-world scenarios, helping students see the relevance and power of these techniques beyond the classroom. By highlighting how professionals, such as journalists, organize information using headings, subheadings, and paragraphs, we can demonstrate the real-world value of these reading strategies. Let's explore how we can make these connections and empower students to navigate the world around them.

One powerful way to showcase the application of chunking and signals is by examining how news articles are structured. Journalists carefully organize their articles into paragraphs with clear topic sentences to chunk information effectively. Headings and subheadings are used to guide readers through different sections and provide visual cues that help readers navigate the content more efficiently. By pointing out these structural elements, we can demonstrate how the same principles of chunking and signaling that students apply in reading can be seen in the real-world creation of news articles.

Here are some strategies to connect chunking and signaling to real-world scenarios:

1. Analysis of news articles: Select news articles that cover a variety of topics and genres. Have students examine how the articles are organized into paragraphs, with each paragraph focusing on a specific piece of information or idea. Guide students to identify the main ideas and supporting details within each paragraph, reinforcing the concept of chunking.

2. Highlight headings and subheadings: Draw attention to the headings and subheadings used in news articles. Explain how these headings provide a quick overview of what each section/subsection is about and enable readers to navigate the article efficiently. Encourage students to identify the main ideas presented in each section based on these headings.

3. Compare multiple sources: Provide students with news articles on the same topic from different sources. Ask them to compare how each source organizes and presents information. Discuss how different writers may use different strategies to chunk and signal information, highlighting the importance of being aware of these variations when reading across sources.

4. Explore other real-world examples: Expand the exploration of chunking and signaling beyond news articles. Show students how other professionals, such as scientists, use headings, subheadings, and visual aids to organize complex information in research papers or presentations. Discuss how these strategies enhance comprehension and clarity for the intended audience.

5. Reflect on personal experiences: Help students reflect on their own experiences in which chunking and signaling played a role in understanding and organizing information. This could be in activities such as following cooking recipes, reading instruction manuals, or navigating a website. Encourage students to share examples and discuss

how these strategies made the task more manageable.

By connecting chunking and signaling to real-world scenarios, we demonstrate their practicality and empower students to apply these strategies beyond the classroom. Students gain a deeper understanding of how these techniques are used by professionals in various fields, fostering critical thinking and helping them become more discerning consumers of information.

In conclusion, the power of chunking and using signals and symbols extends beyond the realm of reading. By connecting these strategies to real-world scenarios, such as news articles, we demonstrate their applicability in our everyday lives. Through the examination of how professionals use headings, subheadings, and paragraphs to chunk and signal information, students can see the relevance and power of these techniques. Let us strive to bridge the gap between reading strategies and real-world applications, empowering our students to navigate the world with confidence and comprehension.

Chapter 10: Differentiated Instruction - Tailoring Chunking Strategies to Individual Needs

Every student is unique, with different learning styles, strengths, and areas for improvement. It is essential for educators to provide differentiated instruction that meets the diverse needs of our students. When it comes to chunking, this means tailoring the strategies and techniques to match individual reading abilities and preferences. By doing so, we can create a personalized learning experience that empowers each child to improve their reading comprehension. Let's explore how differentiated instruction can be applied to chunking and enhance students' reading journeys.

Here are some strategies to implement differentiated chunking instruction:

1. Assess individual needs: Begin by assessing each student's reading abilities and preferences. Use various reading assessment tools, such as running records, reading inventories, or informal observations, to gather information about their

reading strengths, challenges, and preferred learning styles.

2. Offer multiple chunking strategies: Introduce a variety of chunking techniques, such as using headings, highlighting keywords, creating visual organizers, or using gestures. Present these strategies to the whole class, allowing students to experiment and find the techniques that work best for them. Encourage students to reflect on their experiences and share their preferred strategies with the class.

3. Provide guided practice: Scaffold students' learning by offering guided practice sessions tailored to their individual needs. Group students with similar abilities together and provide targeted instruction and practice. For struggling readers, offer additional support during small group or one-on-one sessions, focusing on explicit instruction and guided practice to help them develop their chunking skills.
4. Incorporate technology tools: Utilize technology tools to support differentiated chunking instruction. For example, provide access to digital reading platforms that offer customizable features,

such as adjustable text size, color-coding options, or text-to-speech capabilities. This allows students to adapt the reading experience to their specific needs.

5. Collaborative learning opportunities: Foster collaboration among students with varying levels of chunking proficiency. Encourage students to work in pairs or small groups to share and discuss their chunking strategies. This collaborative environment promotes peer learning, where students can offer support and learn from each other's approaches.

Differentiated chunking instruction allows students to develop their reading comprehension skills at their own pace and in a way that suits their unique learning preferences. By tailoring the chunking strategies to fit their individual needs, we empower students to take ownership of their learning, fostering motivation and engagement in the reading process.

Chapter 11: Independent Practice Chunking with Short Passages 📖🔍🔖

In this chapter, readers will have the opportunity for independent practice of the chunking techniques they have learned so far. The goal is to provide short passages that allow readers to apply their chunking skills in a self-guided manner. By engaging in this exercise, readers can reinforce their understanding of identifying natural breaks and creating effective chunks. A variety of short passages will be presented, encompassing different genres and difficulty levels. This diversity ensures that readers can challenge themselves and practice chunking within various contexts. By encountering different types of texts, readers can fine-tune their ability to extract the main ideas and supporting details within each chunk.

Passage 1:
The Eiffel Tower is a wrought-iron lattice tower located in Paris, France. It was completed in 1889 and has become an iconic symbol of both Paris and France. The tower offers stunning views of the city and attracts millions of visitors annually.

Passage 2:
Climate change is a global issue with far-reaching consequences. It is caused by the emission of greenhouse gases, primarily from human activities such as burning fossil fuels and deforestation. Rising temperatures, sea-level rise, and extreme weather events are some of the impacts of climate change.

Passage 3:
The Mona Lisa is a famous painting by Leonardo da Vinci, created during the Renaissance. It is known for the enigmatic smile and has become one of the most recognized artworks in the world. The painting is displayed at the Louvre Museum in Paris, France.

Passage 4:
Space exploration has led to numerous technological advancements and expanded our understanding of the universe. Missions to the Moon, Mars, and beyond have provided valuable insights into space travel and the potential for human colonization of other planets.

Passage 5:
The Amazon rainforest is the largest tropical rainforest in the world, spanning several South American countries. It is a biodiversity hotspot, home to countless plant and animal species. Deforestation, primarily for agriculture and logging purposes, poses a significant threat to the Amazon rainforest.

Passage 6:
The Olympic Games is an international sporting event that brings together athletes from various countries to compete in a range of sports. The Games are held every four years, with both summer and winter editions. The Olympics promote peace, unity, and athletic excellence.

Passage 7:
Digital technology has transformed the way we live, work, and communicate. The rise of smartphones, social media, and instant messaging has connected people across the globe and made information more accessible. However, it has also raised concerns about privacy, cyberbullying, and the impact on mental well-being.

Passage 8:
The human brain is a complex organ responsible for controlling our thoughts, emotions, and behaviors. It consists of billions of neurons that transmit electrical signals throughout the body. Understanding the brain's functions and mechanisms is a subject of ongoing research in neuroscience.

Remember to practice your chunking skills by identifying natural breaks and creating logical chunks that capture the main ideas and supporting details within each passage. Happy chunking! □

Chapter 12: Independent Practice Chunking with Long Passages 📖

In this chapter, readers will have the opportunity for independent practice of chunking techniques with long passages. The aim is to challenge readers with longer texts where they can apply and reinforce the chunking strategies they have learned. Multiple long passages will be presented, covering various topics and genres to provide readers with diverse reading experiences. By encountering longer texts, readers can practice identifying natural breaks, creating effective chunks, and maintaining focus throughout the passage.

Passage 1:
The Industrial Revolution was a period of significant technological advancements and societal changes that occurred in the late 18th and early 19th centuries. It began in Great Britain and eventually spread to other parts of the world, fundamentally transforming the global economy and way of life.

During the Industrial Revolution, there was a shift from an agrarian, rural society to an industrial, urban one. New inventions, such as the steam engine and mechanical loom, revolutionized production processes and increased efficiency. Factories emerged, creating job opportunities and attracting rural workers to urban centers.

However, the Industrial Revolution also brought numerous challenges. Poor working conditions, long hours, and low wages became prevalent issues faced by workers. Child labor was common, with young children working in dangerous environments. These issues sparked the rise of labor unions and social reform movements.

Despite the hardships faced by many, the Industrial Revolution also brought significant progress. It led to improved transportation systems, the expansion of trade networks, and the development of new industries. The revolution in manufacturing techniques paved the way for mass production and a rise in consumer goods.

Passage 2:
Climate change is a pressing global issue that poses significant challenges for our planet and future generations. It refers to long-term changes in temperature, precipitation patterns, and other aspects of the Earth's climate system.

Human activities, such as the burning of fossil fuels and deforestation, have contributed to the increase in greenhouse gas emissions, leading to global warming. The rise in global temperatures has far-reaching effects, including melting ice caps, rising sea levels, and more frequent and intense extreme weather events.

The consequences of climate change are diverse and impact various sectors, including agriculture, health, and the environment. Changes in rainfall patterns can affect agricultural productivity and food security. Rising temperatures can contribute to the spread of vector-borne diseases and heat-related illnesses. Biodiversity loss and habitat destruction threaten ecosystems around the world.

Addressing climate change requires collective action on a global scale. Efforts to reduce greenhouse gas emissions and transition to renewable energy sources are crucial. Additionally, adaptation measures, such as building resilient infrastructure and promoting sustainable practices, are necessary to mitigate the impacts of climate change and protect vulnerable communities.

Remember to apply your chunking skills by identifying natural breaks and creating logical chunks that capture the main ideas and supporting details within each passage. Happy chunking!

Passage 3:
Artificial intelligence (AI) is an area of computer science that focuses on developing machines and systems that can perform tasks that typically require

human intelligence. Some examples of AI include speech recognition, image recognition, and natural language processing.

AI technologies have the potential to revolutionize various industries, including healthcare, finance, and transportation. Medical diagnoses can be made with greater accuracy and speed using AI, which can analyze vast amounts of patient data. Financial transactions can be monitored and analyzed in real-time, reducing the risk of fraud. Self-driving cars can navigate complex traffic scenarios and improve road safety.

However, the rise of AI has also raised concerns about the impact on employment, privacy, and security. Advances in machine learning and automation have the potential to displace human workers, particularly for jobs that are routine or repetitive. The collection and use of personal data by AI systems raise ethical issues regarding privacy and data protection. The development of autonomous machines and systems raises concerns about cybersecurity and computer ethics.

As the field of AI continues to evolve, it is essential to consider the implications and risks associated with its development and deployment. Ethical guidelines and regulations are necessary to ensure that AI is developed and used in a responsible and beneficial manner.

Passage 4:
The American Civil War was a significant event in the history of the United States, lasting from 1861 to 1865. It was fought between the Confederate States of America, composed of southern states that seceded from the Union, and the Union states, led by President Abraham Lincoln.

The Civil War was fought primarily over the issue of slavery and states' rights. The Confederate states believed in the right to own slaves and sought to secede from the Union. The Union, led by Lincoln, sought to preserve the Union and end slavery.

The war had a significant impact on the United States, leading to the abolition of slavery and the reunification of the country. However, it also resulted in the loss of many lives and the destruction of property and infrastructure.

The legacy of the Civil War continues to shape American society and politics. The struggle for racial equality and civil rights for African Americans has been ongoing and is still a contentious issue. The role of the federal government in relation to state sovereignty remains a topic of debate.

Remember to apply your chunking skills by identifying natural breaks and creating logical chunks that capture the main ideas and supporting details within each passage. Happy chunking!

Chapter 13: Chunking Non-linear Passages 📚

Nonlinear passages are storytelling techniques that deviate from the traditional linear structure of events unfolding in a consecutive and chronological order. Instead of following a straightforward beginning-to-end narrative, non-linear passages present events in a fragmented or non-sequential manner. This can be achieved through techniques such as flashbacks, flash-forwards, or parallel storylines.

In non-linear passages, the story may jump back and forth in time, presenting different moments or perspectives out of order. This can create a sense of mystery, suspense, or complexity as readers piece together the narrative puzzle. Non-linear passages often require the reader to actively engage in making connections and understanding the relationships between events.

These techniques are commonly used in various forms of storytelling, including literature, film, and even video games. Non-linear passages offer opportunities for exploring different viewpoints, enhancing character development, and challenging conventional narrative structures.

Overall, non-linear passages offer a distinctive and captivating way of storytelling by breaking away from the linear progression of events and inviting readers to interpret and assemble the story fragments in their own unique way.

Chunking nonlinear passages can be challenging because these passages often contain bullet points, lists, or diagrams that require specialized techniques for effective chunking.

When it comes to chunking bullet points, it is important to group related points together or break them into smaller clusters. By identifying the main ideas and sub points within the bullet points, readers can create logical chunks that facilitate comprehension.

For chunking lists, readers can group items that share a common theme or purpose. Breaking the list into smaller segments helps readers process and remember the information more easily. Additionally, using numbers or letters to indicate the order or hierarchy of the list can aid in creating logical chunks.

Chunking diagrams involves focusing on specific sections or components at a time. By breaking down the diagram into smaller parts and analyzing each section individually, readers can better understand the overall message conveyed by the diagram.

To further reinforce the concepts discussed examples and practice exercises has been provided for chunking nonlinear passages . Readers can apply the strategies of identifying natural breaks, organizing information into logical chunks, and chunking non-linear passages.

One example exercise involves chunking a news article by identifying paragraph transitions and subheadings. By dividing the article into logical chunks based on these breaks, readers can enhance their comprehension of the article.

Another practice exercise involves chunking a bulleted list from a textbook or guide. Readers can group related points together and create logical segments within the list, using numbers or letters to indicate the order or hierarchy.

By engaging in these examples and practice exercises, readers can strengthen their chunking skills and become more proficient at enhancing comprehension and retention in non-linear passages.

Chapter 14: Overcoming Challenges in Chunking 🎓 📚

Chunking is a powerful study strategy for preparing for tests or exams as it helps you break down information into smaller, more manageable pieces. However, like any learning technique, there can be challenges or difficulties that arise when trying to effectively implement chunking. In this chapter, we will address these common challenges and provide strategies and solutions for overcoming them.

Challenge 1: Identifying relevant chunks of information.
One challenge students often encounter is determining how to break down the information into meaningful chunks. This can be particularly difficult when faced with complex or unfamiliar subject matter. To overcome this challenge, consider the following strategies:

1. Organize information based on themes or concepts: Look for overarching themes or key concepts within the material and use them as a guide for chunking. For example, in a history class, you could chunk information based on different historical eras or events.

2. Use hierarchical structures: Create a hierarchical structure by organizing information from general to specific or vice versa. This can help you see the relationships between chunks of information and facilitate better understanding and recall.

3. Seek guidance from instructors or classmates: If you're struggling to identify relevant chunks, reach out to your instructor or classmates for assistance. They may offer valuable insights or perspectives that can help you chunk information in a more effective way.

Challenge 2: Retaining and recalling information within each chunk.

Even after successfully chunking information, students may face difficulties in retaining and recalling the details within each chunk. To overcome this challenge, consider the following strategies:

4. Employ mnemonic devices: Mnemonic devices, such as acronyms, rhymes, or visualization techniques, can help you associate and remember information within each chunk. Create memorable associations that connect the details, making them easier to recall during exams.

5. Practice active recall: Instead of passively reviewing the information, actively engage in recalling the details within each chunk. Use techniques like flashcards, self-quizzing, or summarizing the information to reinforce your memory.

6. Apply the "spacing effect": Implement spaced repetition by revisiting the chunks of information at regular intervals. This technique enhances long-term retention by repeatedly exposing your brain to the material over time.

Challenge 3: Managing time effectively.
Chunking requires thoughtful planning and organization, which can be challenging when faced with a busy schedule or multiple subjects to study. Here's how you can better manage your time:

7. Create a study schedule: Allocate specific time slots for chunking each subject or topic. This helps you stay organized, ensure sufficient coverage of material, and prevent cramming closer to the exam date.

8. Break chunking sessions into manageable chunks: Chunk your study sessions themselves - aim for

shorter, focused intervals of study with short breaks in between. This helps prevent mental fatigue and enhances concentration and retention.

9. Prioritize effectively: Identify the most important or challenging chunks within each subject and allocate more time and resources to studying those areas. This ensures you make the best use of your limited study time.

By addressing these common challenges and implementing the suggested strategies, students can overcome difficulties and make the most of chunking as a powerful study strategy. With effective chunking, you can break down complex information, retain and recall details more easily, and manage your study time efficiently for improved test performance.

Chapter 15: Home-School Connection - Extending Chunking Strategies beyond the Classroom

To truly empower kids and help them improve their reading comprehension, we must establish a strong home-school connection. When parents and caregivers are involved in their children's reading journeys, the impact and effectiveness of chunking strategies can be amplified. By extending chunking strategies beyond the classroom and encouraging their usage at home, we create a collaborative partnership that supports students' reading growth. Let's explore how we can foster this connection and involve families in the learning process.

Here are some strategies to promote a strong home-school connection regarding chunking strategies:

1. Parent workshops: Organize workshops or informational sessions for parents and caregivers to introduce them to chunking strategies. Explain the benefits of using these techniques and demonstrate how they can support reading comprehension. Provide take-home materials with practical examples and guidance for using

chunking strategies during reading activities at home.

2. Home reading activities: Suggest specific activities that parents and children can engage in together to practice chunking strategies. For example, encourage parents to read aloud with their child, modeling the use of chunking techniques such as pausing at headings or summarizing main ideas. Provide parents with a list of question prompts they can use during conversations about the text, encouraging thoughtful reflection and chunking practice.

3. Communication platforms: Utilize communication platforms, such as newsletters, emails, or digital learning platforms, to share information about chunking strategies with parents. Regularly provide updates on classroom instruction and specific ways parents can support their child's use of chunking techniques at home.

4. Reading logs or journals: Encourage students to keep a reading log or journal where they can practice chunking strategies and reflect on their

reading experiences. Encourage parents to review these logs and provide feedback or ask questions to promote further discussion around the use of chunking strategies.

5. Celebrate progress: Recognize and celebrate students' progress in using chunking strategies both at school and at home. Share success stories with parents, highlighting the impact of these strategies on their child's reading comprehension. Express gratitude for the collaborative partnership between home and school.

By involving parents and caregivers in the chunking process, we create a supportive environment that reinforces the use of effective reading strategies. This collaboration between home and school empowers students with consistent and guided practice that extends beyond the boundaries of the classroom, resulting in improved reading comprehension and greater student success.

In conclusion, differentiated instruction and home-school connections are vital components of promoting effective chunking strategies. By tailoring our instruction to meet individual needs and involving families in the learning process, we empower students to take ownership of their reading comprehension. Let us embrace differentiated instruction and foster collaborative partnerships with families to help our students thrive and achieve their full potential.

Appendix: Additional resources, activities, and worksheets for practicing chunking skills 📚✏️🔢

In this appendix, you will find a variety of resources, activities, and worksheets that will help you further develop your chunking skills. These resources are designed to reinforce the power of chunking and its effectiveness in enhancing your reading comprehension and overall understanding of complex texts.

1. **Reading Rockets** offers a printable Chunking Worksheet that helps students identify important information and break text into manageable chunks. [1]
2. **Teachers Pay Teachers** has a variety of Chunking Activities, including a Chunking Strategy Lesson Plan and a Chunking Interactive Whiteboard Game. [2]
3. **Scholastic** provides a helpful article on Chunking that discusses the benefits of the strategy and offers tips for implementation, as well as a free Chunking Poster that can be downloaded and printed. [3]

4. **Edutopia** offers a video on how to teach Chunking, along with additional resources and teaching tips. [4]
5. **Common Lit** offers a wide range of passages and texts that can be used to practice chunking skills. Their website provides free access to a diverse collection of fiction and non-fiction texts, along with accompanying questions and activities that promote active reading and chunking strategies. [5]

By utilizing these resources, students can enhance their ability to chunk information and improve their reading comprehension skills.

Thank you for supporting your students' learning!

Sources:

1. Reading Rockets - Chunking Worksheet
2. Teachers Pay Teachers - Chunking Activities
3. Scholastic - Chunking
4. Edutopia - Teach Chunking
5. Common lit-Annotate and Chunk Passages